COLLEGE SPORTS TODAY

COLLEGE SPORTS TODAY

ROCK CHALK JAYHAWK!

THE KANSAS JAYHAWKS STORY

GWEN GRIFFIN

CREATIVE EDUCATION

Published by Creative Education
123 South Broad Street, Mankato, Minnesota 56001
Creative Education is an imprint of The Creative Company

Designed by Stephanie Blumenthal
Production design by The Design Lab
Editorial assistance by John Nichols

Photos by: Allsport USA, AP/Wide World Photos,
SportsChrome, and UPI/Corbis-Bettmann

Library of Congress Cataloging-in-Publication Data

Griffin, Gwen, 1957–
Rock Chalk Jayhawk! the Kansas Jayhawks story / by Gwen Griffin.
p. cm. — (College basketball today)
Summary: Examines the history of the Kansas University basketball
program over the past 100 years.
ISBN: 0-88682-991-7

1. Kansas Jayhawks (Basketball team)—History—Juvenile literature. 2. University of Kansas—
Basketball—History—Juvenile literature. [1. Kansas Jayhawks (Basketball team)—History.
2. Basketball—History.] I. Title. II. Series: College basketball today (Mankato, Minn.)

GV885.43.U52G75   1999
796.323'63'0978165—dc21   98-37109

First Edition

2 4 6 8 9 7 5 3 1

"ROCK CHALK JAYHAWK! ROCK CHALK JAYHAWK!"

With this feverish chant, fans of the University of Kansas basketball team let opponents know that they won't be leaving Allen Fieldhouse with a victory. The sturdy brick walls of the arena fairly tremble when the Jayhawks take the floor, and the 16,300 confident voices fall like a hard prairie rain upon the hopes of visiting squads. For more than 100 years, teams have tried to break the spirit of the Crimson and Blue; and for more than 100 years, they have failed. The "Rock Chalk Jayhawk!" chant calls to the stony resolve of Kansas players to rise to any occasion and meet any obstacle head-on. It is also a warning to all challengers that says, "We are the Jayhawks, and today you are in our way."

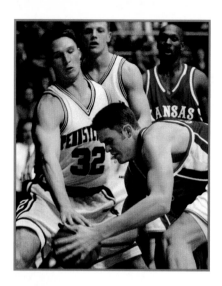

SEVEN-FOOT CENTER

ERIC CHENOWITH

(ABOVE); FORWARD MARK

RANDALL (BELOW)

JAYHAWKS BASKETBALL IS BORN

Long before the first automobile was invented, James Naismith was a physical education teacher in Massachusetts who wanted to develop a game that could be played indoors in winter. In 1891, the head of the school's physical education department asked Dr. Naismith to create a game that was fast and competitive but not as rough as football.

Naismith decided to use a soccer ball for his new game because it was big enough to catch easily. Then he looked for two boxes to use as goals. He couldn't find any boxes in the gymnasium, but the building superintendent gave him two peach baskets. Dr. Naismith attached the baskets to the gym balcony railing 10 feet (3 m) above the floor, and two teams from his physical education class played the first basketball game.

After that first game, Naismith wrote the original 13 rules of basketball, which have remained basically the same for more than a century. Soon basketball was being played by men and women on teams at the YMCA and in high schools and colleges throughout the United States and Canada. No other sport is known to have been invented by just one person. Basketball is also the only popular American game played today that does not have its origins in England or other parts of the world.

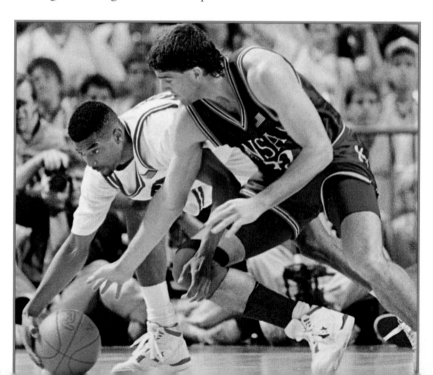

GUARD KEVIN PRITCHARD

CLYDE LOVELLETTE

(LEFT) AND PHOG ALLEN

LED KU TO THE

1952 CHAMPIONSHIP.

The University of Kansas was founded in 1864, during the Civil War, and was supposed to have separate schools for men and women. But when classes began in 1866 with 50 men and five women, resources were so limited that officials couldn't afford to teach men and women separately. So KU opened as the first coeducational institution of higher learning in Kansas.

In 1896, the newspaper in Lawrence reported that "there is talk of organizing a basketball team at Kansas University.... A great many of the members of the faculty and students of the University are playing the game now and it promises to become even more popular."

As talk about the new game continued, Kansas University was looking for a director for its physical education and religious programs. As a graduate of a theological school and with experience in physical education, Dr. James Naismith was a perfect match. He accepted the job.

When he arrived in 1898, Naismith organized basketball at Kansas and held a tournament to select the first team. Jayhawks basketball was born. The team played its first game on February 3, 1899, against the Kansas City, Missouri, YMCA. Although KU lost 16–5, it went on to finish its first season with a 7–4 mark.

In nine seasons, Coach Naismith watched his team play games at the YMCA, at a roller skating rink, and in the basement of Snow Hall on the KU campus. The games at Snow Hall presented a real challenge. The building had support columns in the center of the floor that made it an extraordinarily dangerous place to play basketball. During the 1906–07 season, no home games were scheduled because, as the campus newspaper wrote, "No visiting teams will risk their lives among the pillars."

Naismith ended his coaching career with a 55–60 record. Although he is the only basketball coach at Kansas with a losing record, Naismith's status as the inventor of basketball and the first coach at Kansas has won him a place in basketball history and in the hearts of Jayhawks forever.

BEWARE THE "PHOG"

When Kansas fans watched Forrest Allen set a school scoring record by scorching Emporia State for 26 points in 1906, no one could have imagined what the future would hold for the youngster. Allen's scoring record would last until 1913, but he would find his real place in Kansas history as the team's coach.

After playing for Naismith and helping Kansas to a 12–7 record in 1906, Allen had to drop out of school to work. He held jobs as a basketball and football coach and as a grocery clerk. Then, in 1907, at the age of 22, he agreed to come back to Kansas, not as a player but as the coach.

The 1907–08 season was an important one for the Jayhawks. First, they had a brand-new place to play. The 3,000-seat Robinson Gymnasium was an awesome facility for its time; it had been designed to look like the YMCA in Massachusetts where Dr.

DANNY MANNING

Naismith had invented the game. In fact, Naismith had stepped down as coach to oversee construction of the Jayhawks' new home. On December 13, 1907, Allen christened the new gym with a 44-point victory over Ottawa University.

That season also saw the formation of the Missouri Valley Intercollegiate Athletic Association with Kansas, Missouri, Nebraska, Iowa, and Washington University in St. Louis as members. Kansas would nab the first two Missouri Valley championships under Allen.

Despite his on-court success, Allen knew that he needed more training to become a better coach. In those days, there were no athletic trainers to help the players. Allen believed that a coach who could help his players stay healthy would have an advantage in the game. So Allen left KU again, this time to study in the medical field at the Central College of Osteopathy. After he graduated, he was hired by Central Missouri State College to run its athletic program. His teams won nearly every conference championship.

During that time, Allen umpired baseball games, calling balls and strikes with a big, booming voice that sounded like a foghorn. The students began to call him "Fog," but a reporter who heard the story thought "Fog" was sort of dull. He spelled the nickname "Phog" to give it more flair, and a legend began.

MARK RANDALL (ABOVE) AND

KEVIN PRITCHARD (BELOW)

WERE TEAM CAPTAINS.

During the 10 years that Allen was in Missouri, William Hamilton coached the Jayhawks to five conference championships. He garnered a 125–59 record with

PORTRAIT

NAME: Forrest "Phog" Allen

BORN: November 18, 1885

DIED: September 16, 1974

POSITION: Head Coach

SEASONS COACHED: 1907–09, 1920–56

AWARDS/HONORS: 1950 National Coach of the Year, Naismith Hall of Fame inductee

RECORD: 590–219

Allen, who coached his first Division I game at the age of 22 (still an NCAA record for the youngest coach) is the winningest coach in Kansas basketball history, compiling a 590–219 record (.629 winning percentage) in 39 seasons. His KU teams won 24 conference titles and the 1952 NCAA title. He also contributed to basketball on a global scale by helping to make the game an Olympic sport in 1936 and by serving as an assistant coach on America's 1952 team. One of the founders of the NCAA tournament, Allen was elected to the Naismith Hall of Fame in 1959. Allen Fieldhouse, named in his honor, is still the home court of Kansas basketball.

NAME: Wilt Chamberlain

BORN: August 21, 1936

HEIGHT/WEIGHT: 7-foot-1/250 pounds

POSITION: Center

SEASONS PLAYED: 1956-57–1957-58

AWARDS/HONORS: All-American (1956-57, 1957-58), 1957 NCAA tournament Most Outstanding Player, Naismith Hall of Fame inductee

One of the greatest basketball players of all time, Wilt Chamberlain announced his arrival to college basketball by scoring 42 points in his freshman debut. "The Big Dipper" started off the next season by scoring 52 points and snaring 31 rebounds in one game—a scoring total that still stands as a Kansas single-game record. In just two seasons at Kansas, Chamberlain earned legendary status among college basketball greats.

STATISTICS:

Season	Points per game	Rebounds per game
1956–57	29.6	18.9
1957–58	30.1	17.5

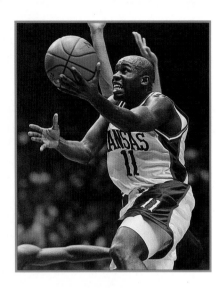

teams that included three All-American players, including Tommy Johnson, who became KU's first All-American in any sport in 1909.

Then, in 1919, Kansas hired Phog Allen again, this time as its athletic director. He wasn't supposed to coach, but when the basketball coach resigned unexpectedly, Allen appointed himself to the position. The team posted an 11–7 finish, and Allen stayed on as coach. In the next 36 seasons, Allen's teams won 22 conference championships and included 62 All-Conference selections and 15 All-Americans. But his influence went beyond the Kansas Jayhawks basketball program.

In 1927, the Joint Basketball Rules Committee voted to limit the dribble to a single bounce. Opponents of this rule formed the National Association of Basketball Coaches, with Allen as its first president. Allen fought to include basketball in the Olympics; he succeeded, and it became one of the sports added during the 1936 Olympic Games in Berlin, Germany. Allen also helped to organize "March Madness," the National Collegiate Athletic Association (NCAA) tournament, which was played for the first time in 1939. In 1950, he was named National Coach of the Year.

CENTER GREG OSTERTAG HAD 258 CAREER BLOCKS.

STARS OF THE 1920S

(ABOVE); THE JAYHAWKS'

1945–46 STARTING

LINEUP (BELOW)

A GOLDEN SEASON

When Phog Allen went to Terre Haute, Indiana, to recruit a young player named Clyde Lovellette, he said, "By your senior year, we are going to win the nationals, and we are going to win the Olympics." Allen had good reason to be optimistic. With the 6-foot-9 and 240-pound Lovellette manning the pivot, the Jayhawks instantly became a top contender for the national title.

"Big Clyde" did not disappoint. In 1949, his first season on the varsity squad, the sophomore averaged 21.8 points and 7.7 rebounds. As strong as an ox, yet surprisingly agile for a big man, Lovellette dominated the paint. By the end of his junior year, he was an All-American and had led Kansas to a 16–8 season mark. By his senior year, Big Clyde was nearly unstoppable, averaging 28.4 points and 13.2 rebounds per game. His stellar performance, along with strong contributions from Robert Kenney and Dean Kelley, sparked the Jayhawks to an 11–1 league mark, good enough for the conference title and the school's first trip to the NCAA tournament since 1941.

Lovellette continued his rampage during the tournament. In a first-round 68–64 win over Texas Christian University, he scored 31 points, tying the single-game record set by North Carolina's George Glamack 11 years earlier in 1941. The Jayhawks then rolled past St. Louis 74–55, with Lovellette pouring in an NCAA-record

44 points. "Clyde's play has made me glad that I'm his coach and not coaching against him," Allen remarked. In the semifinals, Kansas thumped Santa Clara 74–55, and Lovellette again dominated, scoring 33 points—his fifth game in a row with more than 30 points.

The championship game pitted the Jayhawks against St. John's University. KU jumped out to an early lead and never trailed on its way to an 80–63 victory. Lovellette racked up 33 points and 17 rebounds in the game and finished his career with 13 NCAA scoring records. Big Clyde was an easy choice as Most Valuable Player, and Kansas was the national champion.

But KU's golden year wasn't over. With Allen working as an assistant coach on the U.S. Olympic basketball team, seven of his Jayhawks made the team and captured gold in Helsinki, Finland, by defeating the Soviet Union 36–25. "Coach Allen has a lot of things to be proud of," Lovellette said, "but I think the fact that we won these two championships is pretty special to him."

THE HOUSE THAT WILT BUILT

In all of college basketball, the most famous address is in Kansas: Allen Fieldhouse on Naismith Drive.

After playing for 28 years in Hoch Auditorium, the University of Kansas dedicated its new arena, Allen Fieldhouse, on March 1, 1955. A record crowd of 17,228 fans, more than five times as

WILT CHAMBERLAIN

(ABOVE); COACH ALLEN

AND CLYDE "THE BEAST"

LOVELLETTE (LEFT)

many as could sit in Hoch, watched the Jayhawks trample the Kansas State Wildcats 77–67. The victory was the first notched by Allen's successor, Dick Harp, who would lead the Jayhawks from 1956 to 1964. Allen wasn't ready to retire, but he was forced to step down when he was 70 years old, the school's mandatory retirement age. Harp then took the reins and would coach Allen's prize recruit and one of basketball's all-time legends, "The Big Dipper"—Wilt Chamberlain.

The 7-foot-1 Chamberlain dominated college basketball during his two years at Kansas with a career average of 29.9 points and 18.3 rebounds per game. In his first varsity game on December 3, 1956, Wilt turned in the most dominating individual performance in Jayhawks history, pulling down 31 rebounds and scoring 52 points. That 52-point performance still stands as a KU record.

Later, Chamberlain led the Jayhawks to the 1957 NCAA championship game, where they met the North Carolina Tar Heels. Kansas was heavily favored, but the scrappy Tar Heels double- and triple-teamed Chamberlain the entire game. Despite a valiant effort, the exhausted Jayhawks and Chamberlain fell to North Carolina 54–53 in three overtimes. "Somehow we made it through the awards ceremony dry-eyed," said KU guard John Parker. "But once we got in the locker room, we all broke down."

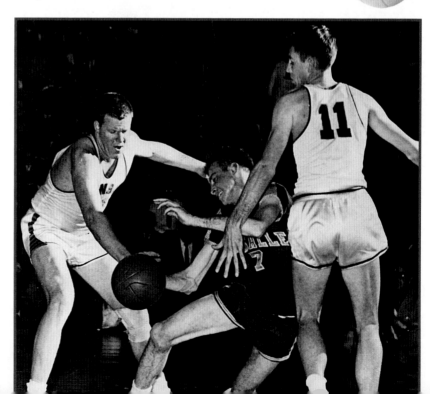

After two years at Kansas, Chamberlain went on to play for the Harlem Globetrotters. In 1959, he signed with the National Basketball Association and became the first player ever to win Rookie of the Year honors and the Most Valuable Player award in the same season. In 14 NBA seasons, Chamberlain won four MVP awards, led the league in scoring seven consecutive seasons, led all players in rebounding in 11 seasons, and never fouled out of a game.

When his No. 13 jersey was retired on January 17, 1998, Chamberlain said that KU basketball "was a great building block for me. It helped me prepare for life." Coach Dick Harp said, "Wilt will be the legend that will live forever." That legend will especially live on in Allen Fieldhouse, "the house that Wilt built."

DREAMS OF ANOTHER CHAMPIONSHIP

In 1964, Ted Owens took over as Jayhawks coach, beginning a career that would include more seasons coached and more victories than any Kansas coach except Phog Allen. His teams won six conference titles and included five All-Americans and 15 academic all-conference players. KU greats such as Jo Jo White, Dave Robisch, and Darnell Valentine all played for the fine Kansas coach.

Owens led the Jayhawks to the NCAA tournament seven times, but the most memorable season during his term was 1973–74. That season, the Jayhawks, led by forward Norm Cook, guard Tom Kivisto, and center Danny Knight, battled through the Big Eight Conference with a 13–1 league record. Ranked seventh in the country, Kansas proudly made it to the Elite Eight in the NCAA

ALL-AMERICAN GUARD

JO JO WHITE SCORED

1,286 POINTS IN HIS

KANSAS CAREER.

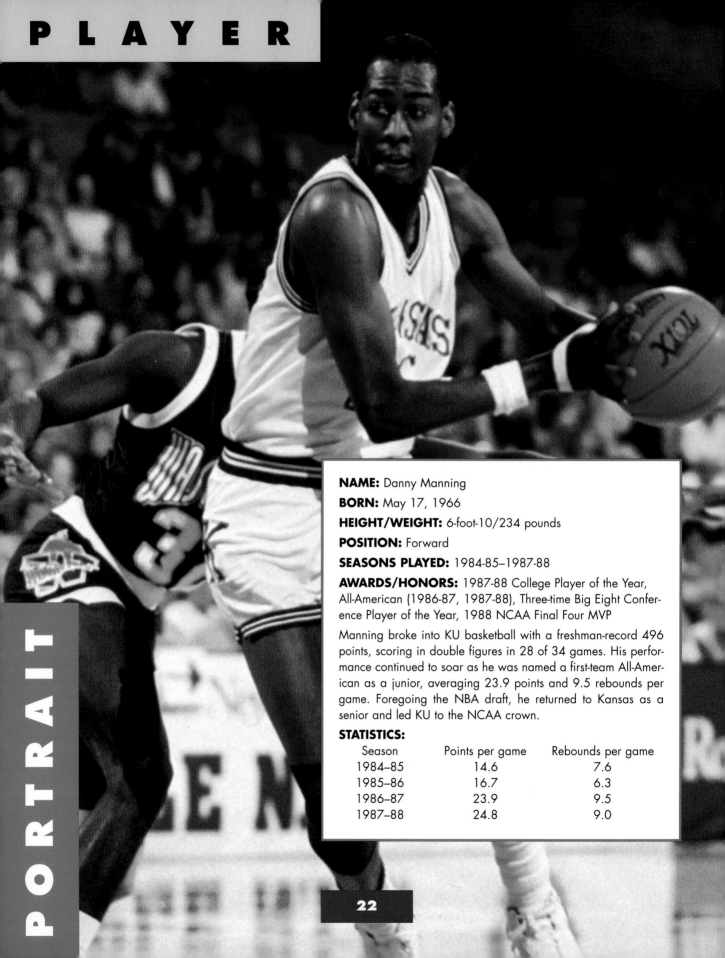

NAME: Danny Manning

BORN: May 17, 1966

HEIGHT/WEIGHT: 6-foot-10/234 pounds

POSITION: Forward

SEASONS PLAYED: 1984-85–1987-88

AWARDS/HONORS: 1987-88 College Player of the Year, All-American (1986-87, 1987-88), Three-time Big Eight Conference Player of the Year, 1988 NCAA Final Four MVP

Manning broke into KU basketball with a freshman-record 496 points, scoring in double figures in 28 of 34 games. His performance continued to soar as he was named a first-team All-American as a junior, averaging 23.9 points and 9.5 rebounds per game. Foregoing the NBA draft, he returned to Kansas as a senior and led KU to the NCAA crown.

STATISTICS:

Season	Points per game	Rebounds per game
1984–85	14.6	7.6
1985–86	16.7	6.3
1986–87	23.9	9.5
1987–88	24.8	9.0

NAME: Eric Chenowith

BORN: March 9, 1979

HEIGHT/WEIGHT: 7 feet/240 pounds

POSITION: Center

SEASONS PLAYED: 1997-98–

AWARDS/HONORS: 1997-98 Big 12 Conference All-Freshman selection

After playing backup as a freshman to the talented Paul Pierce and Raef LaFrentz, the towering Chenowith was expected to become the Jayhawks' primary low-post force. In his first season in Kansas, he pulled down nearly five rebounds a game and demonstrated a remarkable shooting touch for a seven-footer. Although his big frame makes Chenowith an instant defensive presence inside, it is Chenowith's work ethic and unlimited offensive potential that make him a rising star to watch in the Big 12 Conference.

STATISTICS:

Season	Points per game	Rebounds per game
1997–98	6.0	4.9
1998–99	13.5	9.0

CENTER ERIC CHENOWITH

WAS A MAJOR JAYHAWKS

WEAPON IN 1998–99.

tournament and faced Oral Roberts University for the right to go to the Final Four. The game was played at ORU's home court, where the words "Expect a Miracle" were inscribed on the hardwood.

The admittedly nervous Jayhawks got off to a poor start. Scratching and clawing just to stay close, Kansas found itself down seven points with barely three minutes left in the game. Then the Jayhawks put together a furious rally. With one minute remaining, Norm Cook's jumper tied the game and forced overtime. In the extra period, Kansas rode their newfound momentum to a stunning, 93–90 victory.

The incredible comeback left even the Jayhawks amazed, especially Coach Owens. "That was the guttiest performance I have ever witnessed," remarked the stunned coach. Kansas went on to lose to Marquette 61–54 in the semifinals, but the excitement generated by the Jayhawks' fabulous run would live on in the hearts and minds of KU fans.

MIRACLES, MANNING, AND MORE

After two losing seasons under Ted Owens (13–14 in 1981 and 13–16 in 1982), Kansas hired former UCLA and NBA coach Larry Brown to get the Jayhawks back on a winning track. Under Brown, KU went 135–44 over the next five years, including a 55-game home-floor winning streak and the 1988 national championship.

Brown was probably the most superstitious coach in KU history. Coaches on his staff didn't shave on game days. Paisley ties were forbidden, and coaches could never wear the same ties after a loss. During the 1986 NCAA tournament, Coach Brown had his team wear red uniforms, the same color that the 1952 team wore when it won the national title.

While Brown believed strongly in superstition, he also knew it was very good luck to have great players such as Danny Manning, Kevin Pritchard, Cedric Hunter, and Greg Dreiling on his team. During Brown's tenure, the Jayhawks were a threat to capture the national championship every year—every year but 1988, it seemed. Plagued by injuries during the 1987–88 season, KU had given up

hope for an NCAA tournament bid after losing its 11th game of the season to Big Eight rival Kansas State. But surprisingly, the Jayhawks were awarded an at-large

25

bid into the tournament. Many experts thought the invitation was extended only to give senior Danny Manning, the consensus Player of the Year and a two-time All-American, a fitting farewell. Manning, however, was not quite ready to say goodbye.

Behind Manning's phenomenal performances and the solid contributions of forwards Milt Newton and Chris Piper, the underdog Jayhawks pulled out remarkable wins over Xavier, Murray State, Vanderbilt, Kansas State, and Duke to reach the finals. "There were times when we didn't have enough healthy kids to have a practice this season," quipped Coach Brown after the Duke victory. "But here we are, one game away from the championship."

The championship game featured another Big Eight matchup, this time between KU and the Oklahoma Sooners, who had been averaging 102.9 points per game. But the 6-foot-10 Manning dominated the court that night, scoring 31 points and grabbing 18 rebounds to upend the Sooners 83–79. "Whenever they needed a basket, they went to their big man," Oklahoma's Harvey Grant said dejectedly. "That's how they won." The Jayhawks' unlikely championship team was dubbed "Danny and the Miracles."

The 50th anniversary of the NCAA championship game in Kansas City was won by a Kansas team that overcame injuries, beat the odds, and believed in miracles.

THE JAYHAWKS DROVE

ALL THE WAY TO THE 1991

NCAA FINALS.

KNOCKING AT THE DOOR

After the 1988 championship season, Larry Brown left Kansas to take the head coaching job with the NBA's Indiana Pacers. Rumors swirled around Lawrence that Brown's decision had been hastened by an NCAA investigation into rules violations by Brown and his staff. The rumors turned out to be true, and Kansas was hit with NCAA sanctions that included a one-year ban from postseason play.

After reaching the pinnacle of success just a few months before, Kansas basketball was suddenly in disarray and in need of a savior. Looking for advice, KU Athletic Director Bob Frederick called on Dean Smith, the legendary North Carolina coach and a member of the Jayhawks' 1952 national championship team. Smith, the winningest coach in college basketball history, recommended one of his assistant coaches—Roy Williams. No one outside of Chapel Hill had ever heard of him, but it didn't take long for Williams to step into the tradition of winning at Kansas.

The quietly tenacious Williams immediately set about healing the wounds left by the brilliant but reckless Brown. Williams's obsessive attention to detail and love for teaching the game quickly won him the loyalty of both players and fans. "There will be no

RYAN ROBERTSON

(ABOVE) AND RAEF

LAFRENTZ (BELOW)

BRILLIANT COACH ROY

WILLIAMS (ABOVE); THE

TENACIOUS ADONIS

JORDAN (BELOW)

shortcuts," said the determined coach. "We're going to build this thing right."

Williams's first team went 19–12 in 1989 and would have made the NCAA tournament if not for probation. By 1991, though, Williams had the Jayhawks flying high. Standout seasons by guard Adonis Jordan and forwards Mark Randall and Terry Brown drove KU all the way to the Final Four. There, Williams faced off against his former mentor, Dean Smith, and the North Carolina Tar Heels.

The Jayhawks earned a hard-fought, 79–73 victory against a Tar Heels team made up of players that Williams had helped recruit while he was at North Carolina. It was a sweet win, but an emotionally drained KU could not complete the championship journey; the Jayhawks were beaten by Duke 72–65 in the finals. Two seasons later, the Jayhawks faced North Carolina again in the Final Four. This time, however, the Tar Heels took revenge for the 1991 loss, beating Kansas 78–68.

With Williams as coach, Kansas has won more games than any other major college basketball program in the 1990s and has had the longest period of sustained, high-level success in its history. Recent stars such as Greg Ostertag, Jacque Vaughn, Raef LaFrentz,

RAEF LAFRENTZ

and Paul Pierce have all helped set even higher basketball standards in Lawrence. "The only thing left to do here is to win the national championship," said the 1997 All-American Pierce. "Knowing Coach Williams, it will happen soon."

Although the Jayhawks lost the experience of guard Ryan Robertson and forward T.J. Pugh to graduation after the 1998–99 season, Kansas appears to have the ingredients for a strong team once again. Kenny Gregory, a 6-foot-5 swingman, should give the Jayhawks consistent offensive firepower, while guard Jeff Boschee appears to have the makings of the next Jayhawks standout. In the paint, the hulking 7-foot Eric Chenowith has shown promise as a dominating center.

With a talented new Jayhawks squad replacing KU's departed stars, Williams knows his team is ready to claim the crown. "We've been knocking at the door," he said, "and we're going to keep knocking until we've knocked it down."

GREAT KANSAS

GUARDS JACQUE VAUGHN

(ABOVE) AND KENNY

GREGORY (BELOW)